## SURVIVAL SKILLS HANDBOOK

# WEATHER WATCHING

# Bear Grylls

This survival handbook has been specially put together to help young adventurers just like you to stay safe in the wild. Adventuring in all different kinds of weather can be very fun, but all weathers present their own problems. It's important to know how to predict what the weather is going to do, and how to stay safe in heat, cold, rain, wind, and snow. Then you can go into the wild knowing you are prepared for anything!

*Bear*

# CONTENTS

# WHAT IS WEATHER?

Weather means the different conditions outside – whether it's warm or chilly, sunny or cloudy, dry or rainy. Weather affects all outdoor activities, so understanding the weather is a vital survival skill.

## What causes weather?

All the weather conditions we experience are caused by the sun heating the air in different places by different amounts. The oceans also affect the weather (see pages 36–37).

### Rainfall

Falling moisture, such as rain, is called precipitation.

### Sunshine

The sun's heat causes moisture to rise from the oceans, producing clouds.

### Temperature

The temperature is how warm or cold the air is. Snow falls when the air is cold.

## Be prepared!

Prepare for all kinds of weather on outdoor expeditions by bringing several layers of clothing. Take off a layer off if you are hot, and put one on if you are cold. Take a rain, sun, or woolly hat depending on the weather.

You will also need:
1. Waterproof jacket in case of rain
2. Gloves
3. Boots or walking shoes
4. Watch
5. Rucksack

Take these items of kit on all expeditions:
1. Drink and snack
2. First aid pouch
3. Torch
4. Mobile phone
5. Map and compass

# Earth's atmosphere

Weather happens in Earth's atmosphere – a blanket of gases that surrounds the planet. The atmosphere has five main layers: the exosphere, thermosphere, mesosphere, stratosphere, and troposphere.

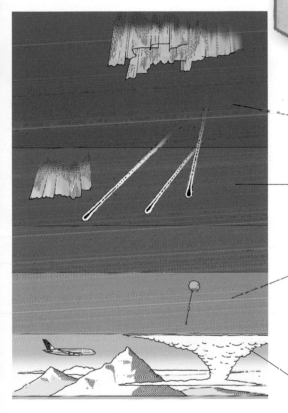

exosphere contains very little gas and fades away into space.

coloured lights called auroras can be seen in the thermosphere (and exosphere).

the stratosphere contains a thin layer of ozone gas, which screens out harmful ultraviolet rays in sunlight. Planes fly in this calm layer.

weather happens in the lowest layer, the troposphere, which also contains most gases.

## Sunscreen

In the 20th century air pollution made the ozone layer thinner, allowing harmful ultraviolet light through. Wear sunscreen outdoors to protect your skin.

# WHAT IS CLIMATE?

Climate is not the same as weather. In many places the weather changes constantly. The climate is the bigger picture – the average weather conditions, as recorded over many years.

## What causes climate?

Three main factors affect climate. The most important is distance from the Equator (an imaginery line that runs around Earth's centre. The sun's rays beat down directly in tropical regions close to the Equator, so the climate here is always hot. They strike less directly in regions further north and south because of Earth's curving surface, so these places are cooler.

## Altitude

Height above sea level also affects climate. The air higher up holds less of the sun's heat, so mountains are cooler than lowlands (see pages 34–35).

## Distance from coast

Coastal regions have a milder climate than places far inland. This is because the sea cools the land in summer and warms it in winter (see pages 36–37).

# Climate zones

Each part of Earth has a particular climate. The main climate zones are shown on this map. Research a region's climate if you plan a trip abroad, so you know what to pack.

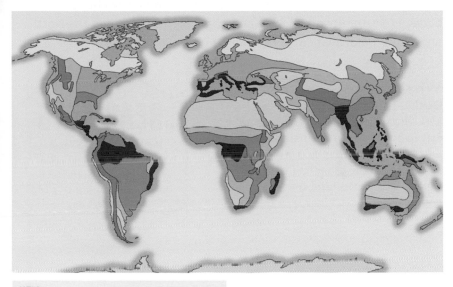

KEY

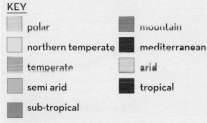

| | |
|---|---|
| polar | mountain |
| northern temperate | mediterranean |
| temperate | arid |
| semi arid | tropical |
| sub-tropical | |

## Microclimates

Small areas such as cities may have a slightly different climate to their surroundings. This is called a microclimate. Cities are warmer because buildings and tarmac trap heat.

## Climate change

Temperatures worldwide are now rising because air pollution is trapping the sun's heat in the atmosphere. Global warming is starting to affect environments worldwide.

# SEASONS

Many parts of Earth have a climate that varies at different times of year. These regular changes are called seasons. They happen because Earth tilts on its axis (an imaginary line between the North and South Pole) as it circles the sun.

## What causes seasons?

Earth tilts at 23.5 degrees on its axis. The tilt always points the same way in space. When one half of the Earth leans towards the sun it has summer, and the other half has winter. Six months later the seasons are reversed.

## BEAR SAYS

Understanding the seasons helps survival experts plan expeditions. Explorers visit the Poles in summer when it's light 24 hours a day.

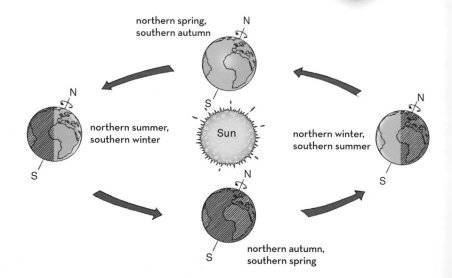

northern spring, southern autumn

N

S

northern summer, southern winter

N

S

Sun

northern winter, southern summer

N

S

northern autumn, southern spring

N

S

## Tropical rainfall
Many parts of the Tropics are wet all year round. Tropical rainforest grows here.

## Wet and dry
Some parts of the Tropics have two seasons – a dry and a rainy season.

## Temperate climate throughout the year
Temperate regions lying between the Tropics and the Poles experience four distinct seasons: spring, summer, autumn, and winter.

### Spring
Broadleaved trees sprout new leaves in spring, when temperatures start to rise.

### Autumn
Broadleaved trees shed their leaves in autumn to prepare for winter.

### Summer
Plants grow quickly in summer, when temperatures are warmest.

### Winter
Broadleaved trees are bare of leaves in winter, the coldest season.

## Polar climate
The polar regions experience extreme seasons. In winter each Pole tilts right away from the sun. It is dark all day and bitterly cold. In summer each Pole tilts towards the sun. It is light all day and all night, but temperatures are still cool.

# WINDS

Winds are currents of moving air. The sun's heat produces winds by heating air in different places unevenly. Air warmed by the sun becomes less dense, so it rises. Cooler, denser air moves in to replace it, making a wind.

## Earth's winds

Warm air rises near the Equator and flows towards the Poles. Cooler polar air rushes in to replace it. This produces circulating wind patterns called wind cells. But winds are also bent by Earth's rotation. This produces regular wind patterns called prevailing winds.

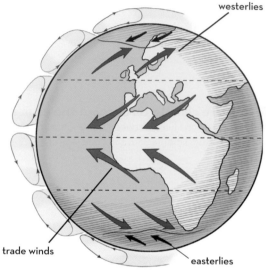

westerlies

trade winds

easterlies

### Wind chill

Wind blows away your body heat, making the air feel colder. This is called wind chill. The tables show how temperatures drop depending on wind speed.

| | Actual temperature °F | | | | |
|---|---|---|---|---|---|
| Wind speed mph | 40 | 30 | 20 | 10 | 0 |
| 15 | 23 | 9 | -5 | -18 | -3 |
| 20 | 19 | 4 | -10 | -24 | -39 |
| 25 | 16 | 1 | -15 | -29 | -44 |
| 30 | 12 | -2 | -18 | -33 | -49 |

| | Actual temperature °C | | | | |
|---|---|---|---|---|---|
| Wind speed mph | 4 | -1 | -7 | -12 | -18 |
| 24 | -5 | -13 | -21 | -28 | -35 |
| 32 | 7 | -16 | -23 | -31 | -39 |
| 40 | -9 | -17 | -26 | -34 | -42 |
| 48 | -11 | -19 | -28 | -36 | -45 |

## BEAR SAYS

When hiking in windy weather, take breaks in sheltered places, such as behind a wall. Avoid exposed places such as ridges, where a gust of wind could blow you off your feet.

## Beaufort Scale

The Beaufort Scale measures wind speeds according to the effects of wind on trees, smoke, buildings, and waves at sea.

### 6 Strong breeze
Large branches sway.

### 0 Calm
No wind, smoke rises vertically.

### 7 High wind
Trees sway.

### 1 Light air
Smoke drifts slowly.

### 8 Gale
Twigs snap. It's hard to walk.

### 2 Light breeze
Leaves rustle.

### 9 Severe gale
Branches break, tiles blow off roofs.

### 3 Gentle breeze
Twigs and leaves move.

### 10 Storm
Trees are uprooted.

### 4 Moderate breeze
Small branches move.

### 11 Violent storm
Widespread damage.

### 5 Fresh breeze
Small trees sway.

### 12 Hurricane
Widespread destruction.

# AIR PRESSURE

Air pressure is the weight of all the air pressing down on us. Differences in air pressure produce weather systems called fronts, which may bring clouds, rain, or storms.

## Measuring air pressure
Instruments called barometers measure air pressure. They also predict the weather. Rising air pressure often brings fine, dry weather. Falling air pressure often produces clouds and rain.

## Highs and lows
Warm air rises, producing a "low", or area of air at low pressure, at ground level. Air swirls around the low-pressure centre and is sucked in and upwards. Sinking cold air produces a "high" of denser air at high pressure. The cold air warms, preventing moisture from condensing, which often produces dry weather.

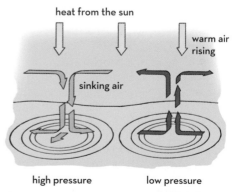

heat from the sun

warm air rising

sinking air

high pressure

low pressure

## Weather fronts

Weather fronts are zones where warm and cold air meet. The front is named after the temperature of the advancing air. These systems are shown on weather maps (see pages 42–43).

## Cold front

An advancing mass of cold air burrows below warm air, which rises quickly. Moisture condenses. Strong winds and showers are often followed by fine, dry weather.

## Warm front

A warm air mass slides over denser, colder air. A sequence of different clouds may be seen.

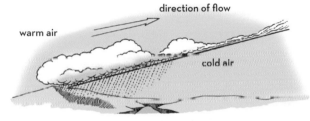

## Occluded front

When a cold front overtakes a warm front, it produces an occluded front. The cold air lifts the warm air off the ground, producing clouds and rain.

# CLOUDS

Clouds are floating masses of moisture – either tiny water droplets or ice crystals. Different types of clouds suggest that fine weather, storms, or rain are on the way, so recognising clouds is an important survival skill.

cumulus

cumulonimbus

cirrus

cirrocumulus

cirrostratus

altocumulus

stratus

stratocumulus

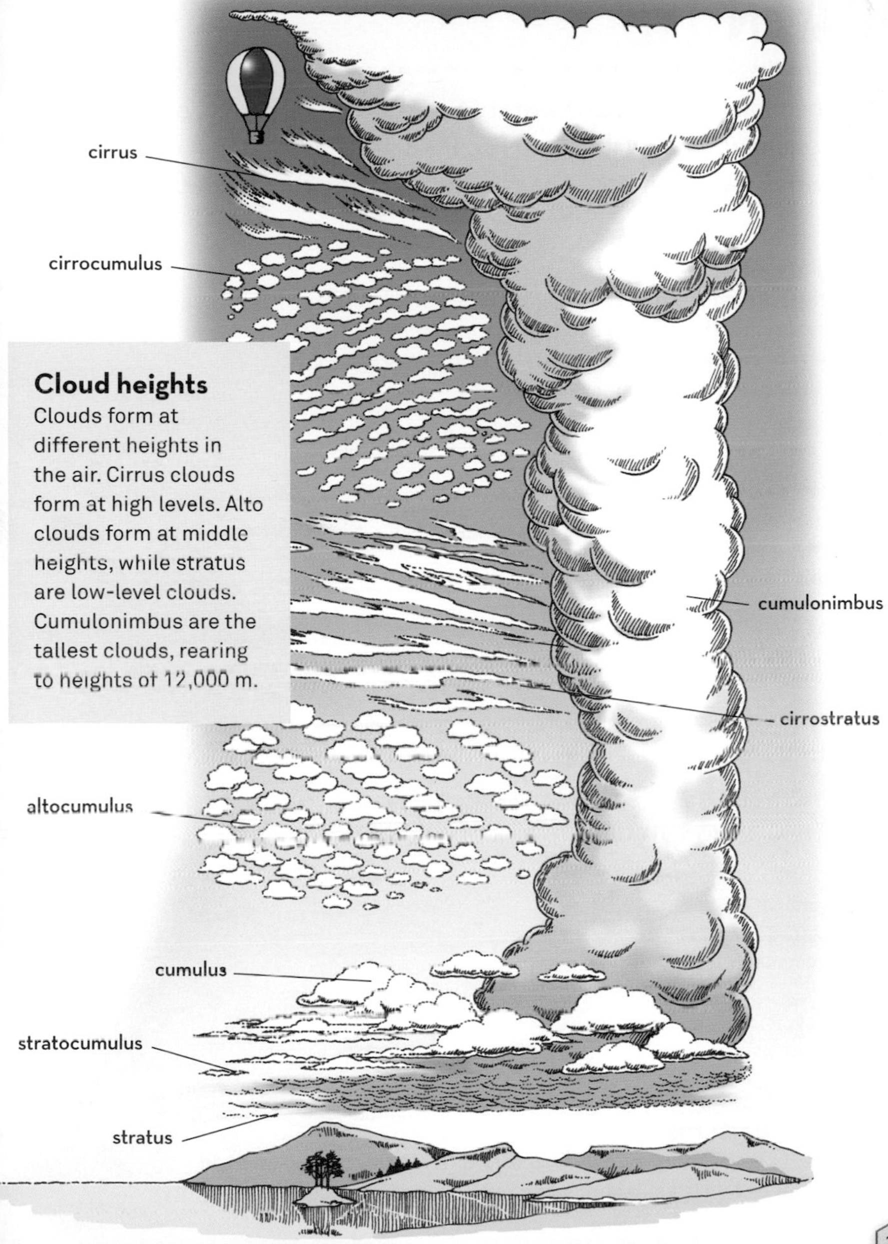

cirrus

cirrocumulus

## Cloud heights

Clouds form at different heights in the air. Cirrus clouds form at high levels. Alto clouds form at middle heights, while stratus are low-level clouds. Cumulonimbus are the tallest clouds, rearing to heights of 12,000 m.

altocumulus

cumulonimbus

cirrostratus

cumulus

stratocumulus

stratus

# RAIN

All the moisture in clouds eventually falls as liquid rain, or icy hail or snow. Falling moisture is called precipitation. For outdoor activities, be prepared for rain even if the weather is fine.

## Why it rains

Tiny floating water droplets in clouds are blown about by air currents. They collide and join to form bigger droplets or crystals. Eventually they get too heavy to float on air, so they fall to the ground.

## Water cycle

Water circles between the air, land, and oceans. We call this the water cycle.

water condenses to form clouds

water falls as precipitation

water vapour exuded by plants

water evaporates from sea

run off from land returns to sea

## Rainfall patterns

Different parts of the world receive very different levels of rainfall. In some places rain is abundant, while regions such as deserts are very dry.

## Rainshadow areas

Mountain slopes facing wet winds blowing off the ocean get a lot of rain. But the air has shed its moisture by the time it reaches the far side of the mountain, producing a dry zone called a rainshadow.

## Wet weather gear

Wet clothing will chill you and can even produce hypothermia. Modern raingear is often made of "breathable" fabric, which allows sweat to pass through while keeping you dry. Avoid wearing jeans, which soak up a lot of moisture and then take a long time to dry out.

## Rainbows

Rainbows form when the sun shines through raindrops. As white light passes through each raindrop it is bent and split into many colours – red, orange, yellow, green, blue, indigo, and violet.

# BEAR SAYS

Line your rucksack with a plastic bag to keep the contents dry. Or buy a plastic rucksack cover – some rucksacks are supplied with a cover.

# MIST AND FOG

Mist and fog are low-lying cloud. When they appear quickly, it's all too easy to lose your bearings. Knowing how to read a compass is vital in these dangerous conditions.

## Mist or fog
If you can see 1–2 km through low cloud we call it mist. If you can see less than 1 km we call it fog.

Golden Gate Bridge, San Fransisco, U.S.

## Forming and clearing
Fog and mist form when moist air cools as it contacts cold surfaces, such as ground or water, and moisture condenses. They often form at night. Fog and mist clear in the morning as the sun warms the air, because warm air can hold more moisture than cold air.

## Map and compass

Use a map and a compass to find your way even in thick fog. This technique is called setting the map.

1. Lay the compass flat on the map. Line up the edge of the compass with the direction you are headed on the map.

2. Turn the round compass dial so the vertical lines on the dial line up with the gridlines on the map, with the red dial arrow pointing north on the map.

3. Take the compass off the map and hold it level. Turn your body around until the red magnetic needle lines up with the dial arrow. The black direction of travel arrow at the front shows you which way to go.

head this way

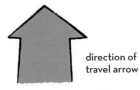

direction of travel arrow

X **BEAR SAYS**

Mist and fog can descend with little warning. In just minutes, all landmarks can be blotted out. Keep calm and get your compass out!

# FLOODS

Flooding can be a danger after heavy rain and thunderstorms. Rainwater quickly swells streams and rivers, turning them into raging torrents.

## Types of floods

There are two main types of floods – river and coastal floods. Rivers burst their banks after heavy rain. Coastal floods strike during high tides, storms, and hurricanes, or they may be caused by tsunamis (giant waves).

## Monsoon rains

Tropical countries such as India lie in the path of monsoon winds that change direction at different times of year. Floods often strike in the rainy season.

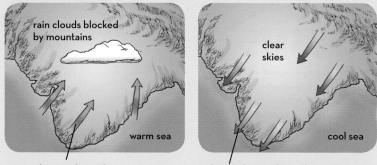

rain clouds blocked by mountains

warm sea

wet southwesterly winds

clear skies

cool sea

dry northeasterly winds

## BEAR SAYS

Never camp in a narrow canyon, gully, or dry stream bed that could flood after heavy rain falls upstream.

## Flash floods

Flash floods strike in deep canyons and valleys below hills and mountains. After a cloudburst, rainwater swells streams, sending a wall of water surging downhill. Water levels rise quickly, sweeping away trees, roads, bridges, cars, and livestock.

## River crossings

Scan for the safest place before attempting a river crossing. A fallen tree may provide a natural bridge, or boulders may form stepping stones. Don't try to cross fast-running water that is higher than your knees.

if there are two of you, link arms or hold onto a backpack

if there are three, link arms to form a circle. Cross with the strongest or heaviest person upstream

a stout stick provides extra support when crossing a swollen stream. You can also use the stick to check the water depth

# THUNDERSTORMS

Thunderstorms are the most common form of extreme weather. In hot, sticky conditions, thunderstorms can strike daily, bringing danger in the form of lightning, high winds, and heavy rain.

### Why thunderstorms strike

Electric charges build up inside thunderclouds as winds cause water droplets, ice crystals, and hail to rub together. The top of the cloud develops a positive charge. The base of the cloud becomes negatively charged, while a positive charge also builds up on the ground below.

## BEAR SAYS

Light travels much faster than sound. To find out the distance of a storm, count the seconds between the lightning flash and the thunder. Divide the number by three to find out the distance in km.

## Types of lightning

When the charge is great enough, electric sparks are released. Lightning can flash inside a thundercloud, between two storm clouds, or from a cloud to the ground.

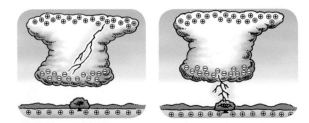

intracloud lightning        cloud to cloud lightning        cloud to the ground

# Places to avoid in a storm

### High ground
Avoid exposed ridges and mountaintops during storms.

### Lone trees
Never shelter under a single tall tree, which could attract lightning.

### Picnic shelter
A picnic shelter offers little protection in a storm.

# Places to shelter

### Car
Cars are fairly safe places. Close windows and avoid touching metal.

### Grove
A thicket of shrubs or low trees is relatively safe if there are taller trees nearby.

### Down low
A gully offers protection against lightning, but may flood after heavy rain.

### Safety tips
Discard metal objects such as walking poles or an umbrella. If you are swimming, get out of the water as quickly as possible.

### Crouching position
Crouch low with your hands protecting your head and covering your ears. If lightning strikes, the current should pass through your feet, not your upper body.

# HURRICANES

Hurricanes are vast, spinning storms that begin out to sea in the Tropics. They are incredibly dangerous, bringing winds of up to 300 km/h, which can uproot trees and rip buildings off their foundations.

## How hurricanes form

Hurricanes form over tropical oceans in warm, sticky weather. As a group of thunderstorms combine, warm, moist air shoots upwards and starts to spiral.

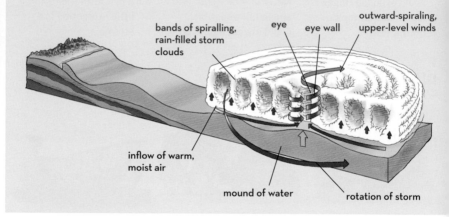

bands of spiralling, rain-filled storm clouds

eye

eye wall

outward-spiraling, upper-level winds

inflow of warm, moist air

mound of water

rotation of storm

## Eye of the storm

From space, a hurricane resembles a whirling catherine wheel of cloud, spinning around a calm central area called the eye.

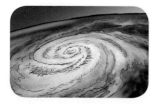

## Storm surge

The low-pressure zone in the eye sucks up water, which heaps up below it. When this mound, called a storm surge, hits the coast, it causes floods.

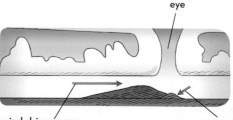

eye

wind-driven surge

pressure surge

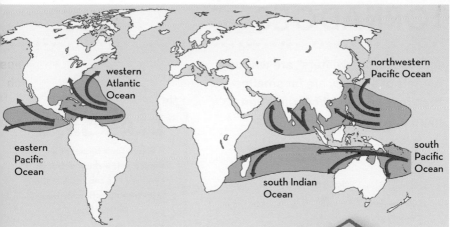

western Atlantic Ocean

northwestern Pacific Ocean

eastern Pacific Ocean

south Pacific Ocean

south Indian Ocean

## Hurricane danger zones

Hurricanes form over warm oceans. In the Indian Ocean they are called tropical cyclones, in the western Pacific they are called typhoons.

## Preparation

Weather experts carefully monitor storms in the hurricane season. If needed, the authorities issue warnings. They may order people to take shelter, or even leave the area.

### X BEAR SAYS

Heed all weather warnings. Never go outside if a hurricane is due. Shelter in a sturdy building, in a basement if possible.

## Storm shutters

People may board up their windows to avoid glass being shattered.

## Devastation

Hurricanes can cause devastation. People are only allowed to return when it is safe.

# TORNADOES

Tornadoes, or "twisters", are whirling funnels of air. They are far smaller than hurricanes but contain even more powerful, spinning winds.

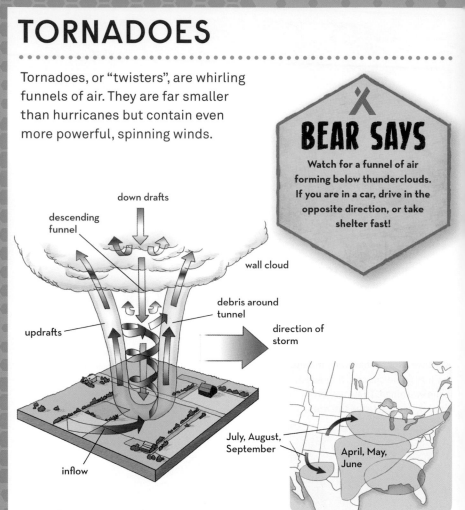

down drafts

descending funnel

wall cloud

debris around tunnel

updrafts

direction of storm

inflow

July, August, September

April, May, June

January, February, March

## How do tornadoes form?

Tornados form over land beneath violent stormclouds called supercells. As warm air rises rapidly and starts spinning, a funnel of whirling air forms below the cloud, and touches down as a tornado.

## Tornado Alley

Tornadoes commonly strike in southern/central U.S., in a wide band called Tornado Alley. Sometimes many tornadoes form – these groups are called swarms.

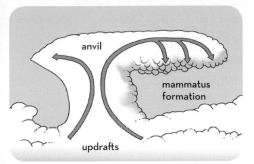

## Mammatus clouds

Weird bulging clouds called mammatus clouds sometimes appear before tornadoes form.

## Dust devils

In deserts, spinning winds can pick up dust to form small whirlwinds called dust devils. Shield your eyes, nose, and mouth from flying sand and grit.

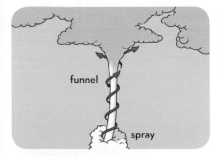

## Waterspouts

Spinning winds at sea sometimes suck up water to form a funnel called a waterspout. These whirling columns don't usually last long.

# SNOW AND BLIZZARDS

Snow forms when moisture freezes in subzero temperatures. When strong winds blow during a heavy snowfall we call it a blizzard.

## Kit and clothing

Wear several layers of warm clothing including a thermal underlayer. The top layer should be waterproof. You'll also need boots, gloves, scarf, and a hat or balaclava to prevent heat loss from your head.

## Why it snows

High in cold clouds, winds blow ice crystals together. They combine to make snowflakes, which eventually get so big and heavy they cannot float, so they drift to the ground.

## Power cuts

Heavy snow can bring power lines down, causing power cuts. Heavy snow can break branches, trees, and roofs.

## Snowdrifts

Wind blows snow into deep drifts that can block roads. If stuck in a car, run the engine as little as possible. Open a window a little to allow fresh air inside.

## BEAR SAYS

In a blizzard, wind drives snow into every gap in your clothing. Make sure you are well zipped and buttoned up before going outdoors.

## Build a snowhole

A snowhole will keep you alive if caught outdoors overnight without shelter. You need a deep snowdrift and a shovel. Dig a tunnel heading slightly downwards and then upwards. Hollow out a space at the end, packing down the loose snow to make a sleeping platform. Use a stick or ski pole to poke an air hole through the roof.

## Snowshoes

Use snowshoes to move over deep snow without sinking. To make snowshoes you need string or cord and green, bendy branches. Bend a long branch into a loop and tie the ends tightly. Tie on smaller cross-struts, then use cord or string to attach to your boots.

## Snow blindness

Dazzling snow can cause temporary blindness. Wear goggles to protect your eyes. Put sunscreen on exposed skin to prevent sunburn.

## Making your own goggles

You can improvise goggles from a strip of cloth, leather, or cardboard. Mark and cut slits for eyeholes. Use string, elastic, or cloth to tie the goggles to your head.

# HAIL, FROST, AND ICE

Hail, frost, and ice are all forms of frozen moisture. Both hailstorms and ice can be deadly, so you have to take great care.

## Hail formation

Hail forms when rising air currents toss ice crystals up and down inside storm clouds. Each time a hailstone rises and falls, new layers of ice are added. Large, heavy hailstones can no longer float, so they crash to the ground.

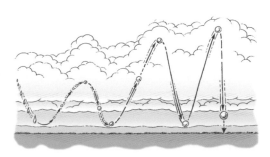

## Hailstones

Most hailstones are no bigger than peas, but they can be as large as golf balls, or even tennis balls. Large, heavy hailstones can shatter car windscreens and glass roofs.

## Hoarfrost

Frost forms when moisture condenses on cold surfaces, such as grass, leaves, and glass, and freezes instantly. Thick hoarfrost coats vegetation when temperatures fall well below zero.

## Hidden danger

Ice forms on lakes and ponds when the temperature falls below zero. Beneath the solid crust is liquid water. Before venturing onto ice, you have to be sure it will bear your weight. Stay away from ice that is less than 8 cm thick.

## How to escape from ice

If you fall through ice, brace yourself for the shock of the cold water. Kick up to the surface and keep your head above water. Swim strongly up to the edge, kick your feet, and haul your upper body out. If you have a knife, use it to stab and grip the ice. Heave yourself out. Roll to safety to drain excess water from your clothes and avoid breaking through again.

kick up to the surface

haul your upper body out

heave yourself out

roll to safety

# COLD CLIMATES

Good preparation is the key to survival in extreme climates. This includes having the right kit and clothing, but also understanding dangers such as frostbite and how to avoid them.

## Polar and tundra

The Arctic and Antarctic are the coldest places on Earth. South of the Arctic lies the tundra – vast, treeless plains that are snow-covered in winter. In summer the snow melts, revealing boggy, waterlogged ground.

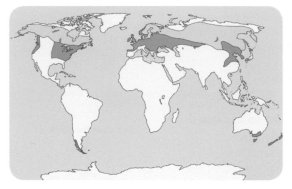

light green shows areas with a northern temperate climate, while dark green shows a temperate climate

## Traditional clothing

Arctic groups such as the Inuit traditionally dress in the skins of the animals they hunt. Undergarments have soft fur next to the skin. Outer garments have fur on the outside to shed snow.

## Modern clothing

Polar explorers wear several layers of clothes made of wool, fleece, or down. Warm air is trapped between layers and next to the skin. Sturdy boots, mittens, and a hat or balaclava are also worn.

## Frostbite

Frostbite occurs when the skin freezes. Fingers, toes, face, nose, and ears are the areas most at risk of frostbite. Frost-nipped skin looks waxy and feels numb. Wiggle your fingers and toes and stamp your feet to keep the blood flowing. Tuck your hands into your armpits. If in a group, pair off and check one another for signs of frostnip. Warm affected areas slowly. In severe cases, see a doctor.

## Hypothermia

Your body temperature can drop dangerously low if you get wet or chilled. This is called hypothermia. Early signs are shivering and lack of coordination. You may feel tired and confused. Get to shelter as quickly as possible. Strip off any wet clothes, and wrap the person in a blanket or sleeping bag. Use your body heat to warm them. Supply hot drinks.

## Keep warm

Exercise such as chopping wood will warm you and keep the blood circulating. But avoid overheating — sweat will cool and chill you when you stop.

## BEAR SAYS

Avoid sitting on snow, which will wet and chill you. Rest on a log or your rucksack instead.

# MOUNTAIN CLIMATES

Mountains have different weather to lowlands. For a start, the air is colder. Mountains are wild, windy places where weather conditions change quickly, so you have to be on your guard.

### Thin air
The air high on mountains is less dense and holds less of the sun's heat. The temperature drops 1° C for every 100 m of height gain. Thin air also holds less oxygen. Some mountaineers breathe bottled oxygen.

### Kit and clothing
As well as cold- and wet-weather gear you will need a rope, helmet, and harness if you go climbing. An ice axe and spikes called crampons on your boots keep a firm grip on snow and ice.

### Mountain zones
Mountains are found on every continent, including Antarctica. The world's highest mountains are the Himalayas in Asia. The area above 8,000 m is called the death zone because no one can survive there for long.

# Glaciers

Glaciers form where packed-down snow spills down from the mountains. These frozen "rivers of ice" are cut with deep cracks called crevasses. These are particularly dangerous when hidden by fresh snow.

# Fog and mist

Fog and mist are common hazards in mountains (see pages 18–19). Low cloud may hide the summits, or mist may form in valleys when the tops are clear. Come prepared to use a compass.

# Avalanche danger

An avalanche strikes when a mass of snow and ice breaks loose and thunders down a mountain. Avalanches can be triggered by heavy snow, midday heat, skiers, or even loud noises. Beware of deep gullies and steep, snow-covered slopes.

If caught in an avalanche, move your arms and legs in a swimming action to keep at the surface. As the avalanche slows, cup your hands over your mouth to clear a breathing space. Spit to find out which way is up, then try to dig and kick your way to the surface. If this fails, stay calm and wait for help.

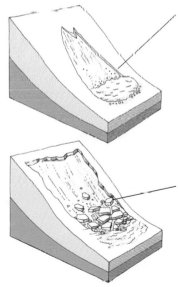

loose snow avalanches occur when light, loose packed snow lies over a solid base on a steep slope. The top layer will slip from a point, often leaving an inverted "V" where it started

when slab avalanches occur, a whole cohesive layer, or slab, of snow slips as one over softer snow, breaking into smaller blocks

# COASTAL CLIMATES

Coasts generally have a mild and rainy climate. The ocean heats up more slowly than the land, but also cools more slowly. This affects temperatures on land, producing cool summers and warm winters.

## Ocean currents

Ocean currents affect temperatures on nearby land. Warm currents flowing from the Tropics warm the lands they flow past. Elsewhere, icy polar currents cool nearby coasts.

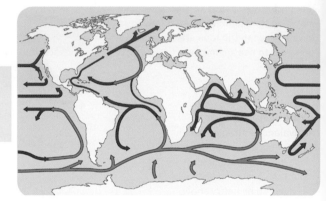

KEY
■ warm currents
■ cold currents

## Coastal breezes

Coast winds blow in different directions by day and night.

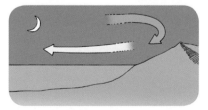

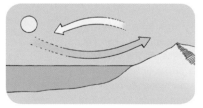

at night, cool air sinks over the land and moves out to sea to replace warmer air that is still rising

by day, warm air rises off the land and is replaced by cooler air blowing off the sea

## High winds

Coasts are generally breezy places because of on- and offshore winds. This wind-blown tree on a cliff edge shows the direction of the strongest winds, which blow in off the sea.

## Coastal fog

Fog often forms off coasts where warm, moist air makes contact with the cold water surface. Thick fog makes it harder for ships to detect hazards such as shoals and rocks.

## Hurricane damage

Tropical coasts are at risk of hurricanes. In warm sticky weather, these whirling storms can blow in, wrecking buildings and driving boats onshore. High seas caused by storm surges can produce floods.

## Rising seas

Sea levels are now rising because of global warming which is melting polar ice (see page 7). In future, this will bring added risk of flooding to coasts and islands worldwide.

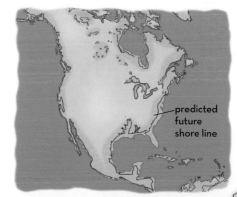

predicted future shore line

# TROPICAL CLIMATES

Heat can be a serious hazard in the Tropics. If the air is moist or humid it will feel even hotter. Germs and disease thrive in warm climates, so you have to work harder to stay healthy.

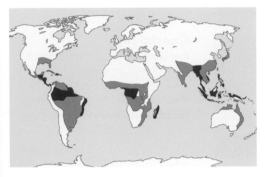

## Tropical regions

Tropical regions north and south of the Equator have a hot, humid climate. Rain falls on most days. The high rainfall allows dense rainforests to grow in this zone.

**KEY**

■ tropical forest
■ subtropical forest

## Jungle survival

Sleep off the ground out of reach of creepy crawlies. Sling your hammock between two trees, and string a tarpaulin above to keep off the rain. Carry dry clothes in a plastic bag and put them on at night. Dry wet clothes by the fire.

## BEAR SAYS

A smoky fire at night will ward off biting insects. Check your legs for leeches after crossing streams.

## Clothing and equipment

A long-sleeved shirt and trousers will help protect you from sunburn and biting insects. Boots guard against leeches and creepy crawlies. Wear boots when crossing streams. A broad-brimmed hat will keep the sun off. Sunscreen, insect repellent, map, compass, and a machete are vital for a jungle trip.

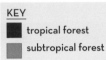

## Prickly heat
This skin irritation is caused by excessive sweating, which chafes the skin and blocks sweat glands. Wash the skin, and put on clean, dry, loose-fitting clothes. Take regular showers if possible.

## Treating sunburn
Cool the sunburnt area with a cold, wet cloth, or apply calamine lotion. Cover skin or wear complete sunblock when next in the sun.

## Heat stroke
Heat stroke is when your body overheats and natural cooling systems fail. Symptoms include fever, weak pulse, high temperature, headache, and nausea. Lie in the shade, remove outer garments, and cool the skin with a wet sponge. Supply cool drinks.

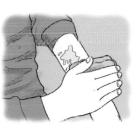

## Purify water
Bacteria thrive in hot, damp climates. Boil water for 15 minutes or sterilise with purifying tablets.

## Sterilise wounds
Cuts and scratches can quickly become infected. Sterilise all wounds with antiseptic ointment or wipes.

## Rest in the shade
Don't rest in full sun. Rig a cloth or tarpaulin to provide yourself with shade.

# DRY CLIMATES

Water is the body's main need. You can last for weeks without food if necessary, but only a few days without water. Finding water is the top priority for desert survival. Rest in the shade by day to reduce water loss through sweating. Work or walk at night, when it is cooler. Avoid strenuous activity that will make you sweat.

## Deserts

Deserts are places where less than 25 cm of rain falls in a year. Most deserts lie in a belt 15–30 degrees north and south of the Equator. Warm, dry air sinking in these zones prevents rainclouds from forming. Deserts may be hot by day but temperatures drop steeply at night.

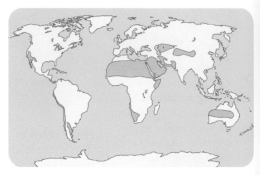

KEY

■ desert areas

## Vital water

You need to drink at least 2 litres of water a day to replace body fluids. In dry climates and survival situations, this can rise to 6 litres. If you don't drink enough you will become dehydrated. As well as feeling thirsty you could get a headache and feel sick, confused, and drowsy. If water is scarce, take small sips rather than gulps.

## Desert shelter

Dig a shallow trench and cover it with a sheet or tarpaulin. Use stones to weight the edges. If possible, rig two layers of cloth, with an air space in between.

## Clothing and kit

Wear thin, loose-fitting clothing and keep well covered. Light-coloured clothing reflects sunlight while dark colours absorb it. A wide-brimmed hat protects the back of the neck. Sunscreen and sunglasses are a must, along with stout boots to ward off snakes and scorpions.

## Where to look for water

Dig for water in the lowest part of a dry stream or river bed. Green plants show where water seeps down cliff faces or trickles underground. Animal tracks may lead to water, while prickly pears and some types of cactus provide liquid.

animal tracks may indicate water is close

## Sand and dust storms

High winds whip up dust storms, which fill the air with sand or grit. Wear goggles and a face mask if you have them, or wrap a cloth around your head and cover your eyes, nose, and mouth. Head for shelter such as a car, tent, or rocks.

goggles

face protection

dust mask

# WEATHER FORECASTING

Knowing what the weather will bring is useful for anyone who spends time outdoors. Checking the forecast is a vital part of planning for all outdoor expeditions.

## Weather stations and aircraft

Weather stations all over the world provide data on temperatures, cloud cover, winds, and rainfall. Aircraft and balloons gather data about conditions high in the air.

## Satellites

Satellites use radar and other sensing equipment to track clouds, storms, and hurricanes. This helps experts to predict which way storms are moving, so they can issue warnings.

## Weather buoys

Weather ships and buoys provide information about conditions at sea, such as wind and waves. This is used for land and shipping forecasts.

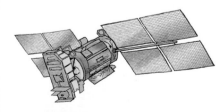

## BEAR SAYS

Compare weather forecasts on different websites with the actual conditions on the day to find out which sites provide the most accurate forecasts.

isobars are lines that connect areas with the same air pressure. Strong winds blow where these lines appear close together

## Weather maps

Weather maps show air pressure, weather fronts, and temperatures. They also give information on wind speeds and directions. Many maps include symbols for different types of weather, such as sunshine and storms.

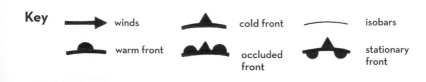

**Key**

→ winds

▲▲▲ cold front

— isobars

●●● warm front

▲●▲● occluded front

▲●▲ stationary front

# WEATHER RECORDS

What are the Earth's hottest, coldest, windiest, and wettest places? This map shows the locations of the world's most extreme weather, based on records that go back over 150 years.

## Strongest wind

The fastest winds on Earth blow inside tornadoes. The fastest speed ever clocked was 486 km/h, in a tornado that hit Oklahoma City, U.S. in 1999.

## Most snow in 24 hours

Silver Lake near Denver, U.S. received 2.4 m of snow in one day during a blizzard in 1921.

## Hottest place

The highest temperature ever recorded was 56.7°C. It was recorded in Death Valley, western U.S. in July 1913.

## Driest place

The driest spot on Earth is the Atacama Desert near the southern tip of South America. The polar regions are also very dry.

## Windiest place

Earth's windiest place is Commonwealth Bay in eastern Antarctica.

## Highest annual rainfall

The town of Cherrapunji in northern India recorded 26,470 mm) of rain in 1860–61. The nearby town of Mawsynram holds the modern record, receiving up to 11,873 mm of rain per year.

## Largest hailstone

In 1986 a hailstone that fell in Gopalganj, Bangladesh weighed up to 1 kg and killed 92 people.

## Highest rainfall in a day

Cilaos on the island of Reunion in the Indian Ocean received 1,825 mm of rain in 24 hours during a hurricane in 1966.

## Coldest place

The coldest temperature ever recorded was -89°C. It was recorded at Vostock Base in Antarctica.

# GLOSSARY

**Air pressure** The weight of all the air pressing down on Earth, pulled by gravity.

**Altitude** The height above sea level.

**Atmosphere** The layer of gases that surrounds the Earth.

**Avalanche** When a mass of snow and rock slips down a mountain.

**Axis** An imaginary line between the North and South Poles.

**Barometer** An instrument used to measure air pressure and predict weather.

**Climate** The regular pattern of weather experienced in a region over many years.

**Cloudburst** A sudden, very heavy shower.

**Condensation** When water changes from a gas into a liquid.

**Dehydrated** When the body lacks water because of failure to drink enough liquid.

**Equator** An imaginary line around the Earth's middle.

**Evacuation** When the authorities order everyone to leave an area.

**Evaporation** When water changes from a liquid into a gas.

**Flash flood** When a stream or river bursts its banks after heavy rain.

**Glacier** A mass of ice that is slowly sliding downhill.

**Global warming** Rising temperatures worldwide, caused by air pollution.

**Hemisphere** One half of the Earth, as divided by the Equator.

**Hurricane** A huge spinning storm with very powerful winds.

**Hypothermia** When the body loses heat in cold temperatures.

**bars** Lines on a weather map joining areas of equal air pressure.

**croclimate** A small area which has a different climate to its surroundings.

**isture** Wetness.

**nsoon** Changeable winds which bring rain at certain times of year.

**cluded front** Region where a cold front overtakes a warm front, producing uds and rain.

**one layer** A layer of ozone gas in the atmosphere that screens out harmful raviolet rays in sunlight.

**les** The area around the North and South Poles, also called the polar regions.

**ecipitation** When moisture falls from clouds as rain, sleet, snow, or hail.

**evailing** The main wind that blows in a region.

**inshadow** A dry area located on the side of a mountain away from wet winds.

**et** Slushy snow that has partly melted while falling.

**rm surge** A mound of water that piles up below the eye of a hurricane.

**arm** A group of tornadoes.

**mperate** A mild climate.

**rnado** A funnel of spinning air that forms below a thundercloud.

**posphere** The lowest layer of the atmosphere, where weather happens.

**nami** A giant wave, usually caused by an undersea earthquake.

**ter vapour** Moisture in the form of an invisible gas.

**ather front** A region where warm air meets cold air.

**nd cell** A large-scale wind circulation pattern.

# Discover more amazing books in the Bear Grylls series:

Perfect for young adventurers, the *Survival Skills* series accompanies an exciting range of colouring and activity books. Curious kids can also learn tips and tricks for almost any extreme situation in *Survival Camp*, explore Earth in *Extreme Planet*, and discover some of history's greatest explorers in the *Epic Adventures* series.

Conceived by Weldon Owen, an imprint of King's Road Publishing, in partnership with Bear Grylls Ventures

Produced by Weldon Owen, an imprint of King's Road Publishing
Suite 3.08 The Plaza, 535 King's Road,
London SW10 0SZ, UK

WELDON OWEN
Designer Shahid Mahmood
Editorial Claire Philip, Susie Rae, Lydia Halliday
Contributor Jen Green
Illustrators Bernard Chau, Stuart Jackson-Carter
Cover photograph copyright © by Ben Simms 2017

## Disclaimer

Weldon Owen and Bear Grylls take pride in doing our best to get the facts right in putting together the information in this book, but occasionally something slips past our beady eyes. Therefore we make no warranties about the accuracy or completeness of the information in the book and to the maximum extent permitted, we disclaim all liability. Wherever possible, we will endeavour to correct any errors of fact at reprint.

Kids – if you want to try any of the activities in this book, please ask your parents first! Parents – all outdoor activities carry some degree of risk and we recommend that anyone participating in these activities be aware of the risks involved and seek professional instruction and guidance. None of the health/medical information in this book is intended as a substitute for professional medical advice; always seek the advice of a qualified practitioner.

A WELDON OWEN PRODUCTION. AN IMPRINT OF KINGS ROAD PUBLISHING
PART OF THE BONNIER PUBLISHING GROUP.